B is for Berkshires

WRITTEN BY JOAN DURIS   PHOTOGRAPHS BY GILLIAN JONES

ISLANDPORT ||||||| PRESS
Published by Islandport Press
P.O. Box 10
Yarmouth, Maine 04096
books@islandportpress.com
www.islandportpress.com

ISBN: 978-1-939017-51-2
Library of Congress Control Number: 2014911179
Printed in the United States by Versa Press

For my husband, Bob, and my brothers, Michael and Jerry—fellow explorers through life. A huge thank-you to my Concord critique group friends who shared my journey toward publication. And a special thanks to new friends in the Berkshires, who shared fun bits of information for this book.—JOANNIE

For Mom, Dad, Aunt Shirley, Professor Johns, Jonathan, Sally, Celia, Erica, Sarah, and all my friends and loved ones who have supported my photography over the years. Special thanks to The Berkshire Eagle *for allowing reprint rights for some of the photographs in this book.* —GILLIAN

DRAPED ACROSS far western Massachusetts are the hills and valleys of what the Mahican Indians called *Housatonnuck*, or "a place over the mountains." The Berkshires owe their haunting landscape to a complex history of colliding continents, shallow seas, and grinding glaciers.

Half a billion years ago, a collision between Africa and North America created massive folds in the earth. Huge slabs of rock thrust westward, piling into a mountain range that was once higher than the Rocky Mountains. Time whittled down the mountains, and glaciers further sculpted the land.

This forty-eight-mile-long strip of Massachusetts has more than 100,000 acres of protected land. Mount Greylock, the state's highest peak, dominates the north. Four major rivers tumble and flow through its valleys. Unique and diverse habitats are home to many rare plants and animals. The natural beauty, quaint towns, and thriving cultural community draw visitors throughout the year.

Outdoor adventures and laughter abound— we're having a blast in nature's playground.

Explore the Berkshires! Fish, swim, boat, or float on the area's waterways. Splash down rivers on a whitewater rafting trip. Zip through trees on a canopy tour, or head for an adventure park.

Grab a backpack for a camping trip and discover nature up close. Hike a stretch of the Appalachian Trail. Wander along backcountry trails in state parks and forests. Find hidden treasures in geocaches and letterboxes. Picnic on Taconic or Hoosac peaks with valley views at your feet.

Outdoor adventures don't stop when the snow starts. Hit the slopes for snowboarding, skiing, tubing, and sledding. Or experience the wilderness on snowmobiles, snowshoes, and cross-country skis. No matter what the season, there is always an adventure waiting for you in the Berkshires.

Photo: Grace Smith at Taconic Golf Course, Williamstown

A is for Adventure

A is also for agriculture, auctions, antiques, arrowheads, Ashintully Gardens, asters, actors, and authors.

Along the trails,
our bicycles soar,
so many places
for us to explore!

Strap on a helmet and pedal your way through the Berkshires. If you don't have a bike—no problem. Many companies in the area offer bicycle rentals and suggest routes to travel.

The Ashuwillticook (ash-oo-WILL-ti-cook) Rail Trail is a popular bicycling path. This paved, eleven-mile-long trail hugs the Hoosic River and Cheshire Reservoir. Look for painted turtles along the way. Listen for the "quack" of wood frogs in the spring.

If you enjoy mountain biking, head for ski areas such as Jiminy Peak, in Hancock, and Stump Sprouts, in Hawley. Or you can pick up a map and explore the mountain biking trails in Savoy Mountain State Forest. Scenic bike routes also wind their way across back roads in the Berkshire Hilltowns.

Photo: Ashuwillticook Rail Trail

B is for Bicycling

B is also for Bridge of Flowers, Bay State Winter Games, barns, birches, beavers, black bears, and blueberries.

*Water seeps through
cracks and soil,
forming caves
with patient toil.*

Another world hides under the Berkshire Hills: a world of caves! Great Radium Springs Cave is the longest cave in Massachusetts—1,605 feet. On private property in Pittsfield, it's only open for special caving events.

Berkshire caves have hidden illegal activity for hundreds of years. Gill Belcher used a cave under Bung Hill in Great Barrington to counterfeit silver coins. He was captured at gunpoint and sentenced to hang in 1772. Area caves were also hideouts during the Revolution. Fleeing soldiers sometimes hid in hillside caves for years.

Today, you can explore caves on the Ledges Trail at Bartholomew's Cobble in Sheffield. Or check out the caves carved by Hudson's Brook near the Natural Bridge in North Adams. Bring a flashlight and friends for Baker's Quarry Cave in Lanesborough. It's 232 feet long!

Photo: Ledges Trail, Bartholomew's Cobble in Sheffield

C is for Caves

C is also for camping, cellar holes, cows, cottages, the Clark Art Institute, Chesterwood, cliffs, and chasms.

Dairy farmers make simple vows: Cherish the land, keep happy cows.

As caretakers of the land, dairy farmers use *sustainable* farming practices. This means they enrich the soil, putting more into the land than they take out. Cows produce tons of manure, providing free fertilizer for the fields.

Throughout the Berkshires, these farmers provide more than just milk, cheese, and other dairy products. Visitors are welcome at Cricket Creek Farm, in Williamstown, where they also sell baked goods and vegetables, and raise pigs and chickens. Signs point you to the animals. All their cows have names, and calves are bottle-fed twice a day.

Cows rule at High Lawn Farm in Lee—they have waterbeds and milking robots! Cows choose when they want to be milked. They even activate a giant, rolling brush whenever they want a good scrubbing.

Photo: Cricket Creek Farm

D is for Dairy

D is also for downhill skiing, dance, deer, drumlins (glacial landform), dams, and Deerfield River.

Wings spread wide,
hunting prey,
an eagle looks
for a fish buffet.

It takes a lot of work to raise eaglets. Bald eagle parents build nests as big as twelve feet high and more than eight feet wide! Busy parents feed demanding eaglets up to two pounds of fish per day.

Loss of habitat and pollution threatened our national bird. By the 1980s, there hadn't been breeding eagles in Massachusetts for eighty years. Then they returned home through conservation and relocation efforts. Today these regal birds once again soar overhead on their seven-foot wingspans.

The state's 2014 spring eagle survey located forty-one active nests. Spotters found three nests in the Berkshires: at Lake Buel, Laurel Lake, and Onota Lake. Perhaps you'll find the next huge nest as eagles claim new territory across the area.

Photo: Hoosac Lake, Cheshire

E is for Eagle

E is also for entertainment, education, erosion, erratics (glacial rocks), echinacea (flower), elk, and egret.

*Nature's paint
splashes each tree.
How many colors
can you see?*

October hikes in the Berkshires mean crisp air and the crunch of leaves underfoot. Red and gold maples glow overhead in the sunlight. And on those breezy-day hikes, gusty winds bring leaf showers.

Slow drives on back roads often lead to unexpected bursts of color. Avoid long lines of leaf-peepers on crowded highways. Meander instead on scenic byways through deep valleys and open farmland. Stop for a picnic on a hillside cloaked in brilliant fall foliage.

North Adams celebrates autumn in style. Their weeklong Fall Foliage Festival includes three parades and a hunt for colored-paper leaves hidden throughout the northern Berkshires. Ashfield and Conway offer unique sports during their fall festivals. Try pumpkin bowling, or watch a skillet toss!

F is for Fall Foliage

F is also for farmers' markets, Florida (the town!), fly fishing, fireflies, foxes, fishers, ferns, and fog.

*Windswept vistas
are what we seek,
making our way
toward Greylock's peak.*

At 3,491 feet, Mount Greylock is the state's highest peak. Scientists call Greylock an inland island. Its geology, climate, and vegetation are different from its surroundings. The summit is battered by cold, wet, and windy weather. Many rare plants and animals call these harsh conditions home. It's the only place in the state where blackpoll warblers nest.

Bascom Lodge and the War Memorial Tower are famous summit landmarks. Five 1,600-watt bulbs light the tower's beacon.

Hike to the summit when the sun is low. You might glimpse a ghostly shadow with a rainbow halo. Called a "Brocken spectre," this rare sight only appears in misty weather. Or join more than two thousand hikers in Adams for the annual Mount Greylock Ramble. You can earn prizes on this traditional Columbus Day hike!

Photo: Veterans War Memorial Tower, Mount Greylock

G is for Greylock

G is also for galleries, Gilded Age, gorges, granite, glens, glacial potholes, and Guilder Pond.

H is for Hoosac Tunnel

*Trains couldn't climb
a mountain so steep,
so men blasted a tunnel,
long, dark, and deep.*

In the 1800s, Boston companies wanted a direct route to ship goods west, but the Hoosac Range blocked train travel across the Berkshires. So in 1851, work started on the Hoosac Tunnel between the towns of Florida and North Adams.

Miners often wore raincoats to work. This is because it was constantly raining inside the mountain! Seams in the rocks held millions of gallons of water. Blasts sometimes released floods, which meant workers had to run for their lives. During the twenty-four years it took to build the 4.74-mile-long tunnel, 136 workers died in floods, fires, explosions, and tunnel collapses.

Drills, mining, and surveying techniques invented at Hoosac are still used today. A dozen freight trains, including two-mile-long truck trains, continue to wheel their way through the tunnel every day.

Photo: Western Portal, Hoosac Tunnel, North Adams

H is also for hairpin turns, Hilltowns, haystacks, hawks, and Housatonic River.

I is for Ice

*Water transforms
with winter's cold,
into frozen sculptures,
bright and bold.*

Winter storms, charging in from the west, dump their snow on the Berkshires. The area averages more snowfall than the rest of the state, and it also has its share of ice storms, with sleet and freezing rain.

Low-lying clouds often hide the higher elevations on ridges and mountaintops. In the winter, this creates freezing fog. Water droplets in the fog turn into rime ice when they touch solid objects.

Soft rime ice forms in calm weather. The fog freezes into delicate sculptures of white, feathery ice needles. Hard rime ice forms in windy weather. Fog freezes on the wind-facing side of objects, building up into a wintery comb. The teeth of the comb point in the direction of the wind.

Photo: Eastern summit of Mount Greylock, overlooking Adams

I is also for icicles, ice jams, interpretive trails, inns, and ice cream.

J is for Jacob's Pillow

Tippity-tap,
heels brush in,
step over step,
shuffle and spin.

Ballet. Tap. Hip-hop. Jazz. Dancers and choreographers from around the world flock to Jacob's Pillow, in Becket, for the summer Dance Festival. Feel the beat at hundreds of joyful and inspiring (and free!) performances.

Students at several local schools use dance to understand a wide range of new concepts. *Jacob's Pillow Curriculum in Motion* programs match artists with teachers. Students may use dance to explore anything from science and math problems to the differences between cultures.

Dreams can come true at Jacob's Pillow. Slaves dreaming of freedom stopped here on the Underground Railroad. Ted Shawn's dream of a dance retreat and school began when he purchased the property in 1931. Share their dreams by having your picture taken on the famous, pillow-shaped rock that gives Jacob's Pillow its name.

Photo: Inside/Out performance at Jacob's Pillow. Used with permission from Emily Schoen / Schoen Movement Company. Courtesy Jacob's Pillow Dance Festival.

J is also for Jones Nose Trail, jasmine, jewelry, jute, jugglers, junco, and Jug End Mountain.

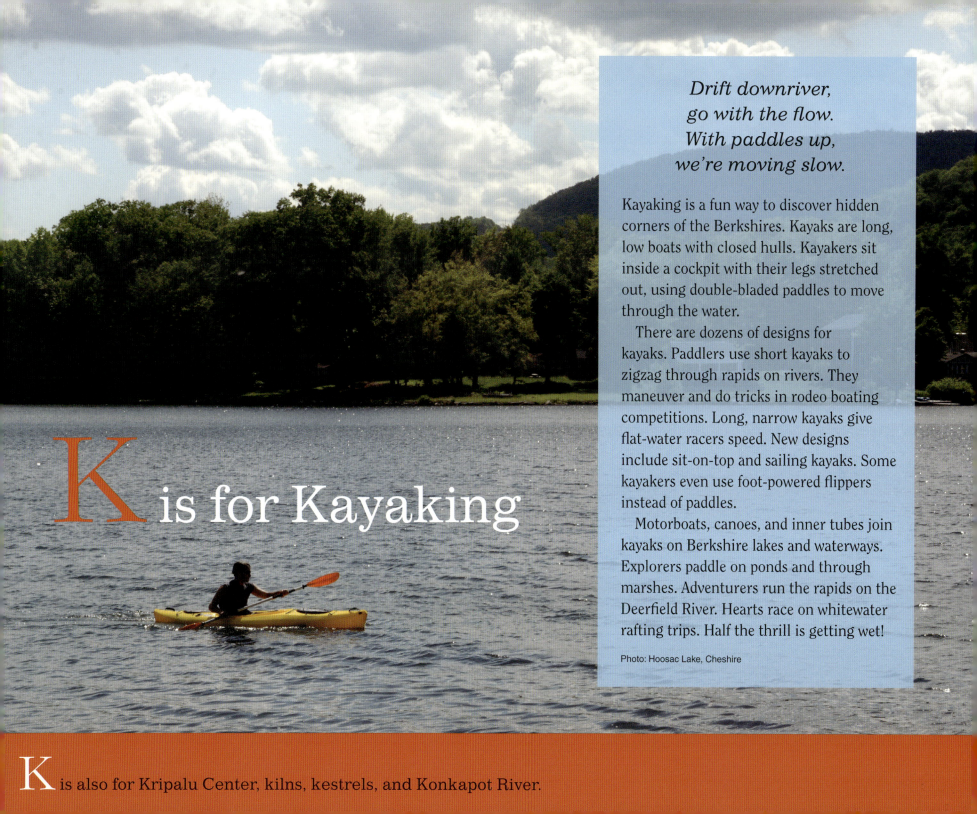

Drift downriver,
go with the flow.
With paddles up,
we're moving slow.

Kayaking is a fun way to discover hidden corners of the Berkshires. Kayaks are long, low boats with closed hulls. Kayakers sit inside a cockpit with their legs stretched out, using double-bladed paddles to move through the water.

There are dozens of designs for kayaks. Paddlers use short kayaks to zigzag through rapids on rivers. They maneuver and do tricks in rodeo boating competitions. Long, narrow kayaks give flat-water racers speed. New designs include sit-on-top and sailing kayaks. Some kayakers even use foot-powered flippers instead of paddles.

Motorboats, canoes, and inner tubes join kayaks on Berkshire lakes and waterways. Explorers paddle on ponds and through marshes. Adventurers run the rapids on the Deerfield River. Hearts race on whitewater rafting trips. Half the thrill is getting wet!

Photo: Hoosac Lake, Cheshire

K is for Kayaking

K is also for Kripalu Center, kilns, kestrels, and Konkapot River.

*Llamas amble
down well-worn paths,
picking spots
for dusty baths.*

Llamas are camel cousins with long, banana-shaped ears—but they don't have humps. Like their cousins, llamas need little water and graze on a variety of plants. Adult llamas can be up to six feet tall and weigh 450 pounds. They often hum to each other. Males sometimes spit stomach goo, kick, or neck-wrestle to determine who's boss. Females usually just spit to set limits on feisty males.

Berkshire llama farms have herds for breeding and show. Guard llamas protect sheep and alpacas from coyotes and other predators. Gentle and curious, llamas enjoy being around people and can be trained as pack animals. But they can be stubborn! Give them too much weight, and they won't budge until you lighten the load.

Photo: Zabu, an eleven-year-old llama at Sweet Brook Farm, Williamstown

L is for Llama

L is also for legends, literary landmarks, limonite (mineral), laurel, ledges, and lakes.

M is for Museum

*Cultural treasures,
so much to learn—
new discoveries
at every turn!*

Past, present, and future: Museums across the Berkshires allow you to encounter history or experiment with new ideas. At the Clark Art Institute in Williamstown, Old Masters of American and European art can be experienced in new ways through digital apps and multimedia guides. Be amazed at the MASS MoCA (Museum of Contemporary Art) by modern, colossal exhibits in its football field–size gallery.

Go back in time by playing with nineteenth-century toys at the Hancock Shaker Village, an outdoor history museum. Ride a vintage train at the Berkshire Scenic Railway Museum. Become a mad scientist at the Berkshire Museum. Enjoy hands-on activities, art camps, concerts, and more at area museums. What will *you* discover?

Photo: Reflective pools, Clark Art Institute, Williamstown

M is also for Mahicans, maples, music, mountains, marshes, moose, and the Mohawk Trail.

N is for Notch

Hills hug our route—
look left, look right;
we pass through a notch
in shadowed sunlight.

A *notch* is a narrow route between mountain peaks. Notches are also called passes, gaps, or saddles. Native Americans, settlers, and then motorists followed river valleys to cross the steep Hoosac Range from the east.

The Mohawk Trail (Route 2) cuts through Cold River Notch and Florida Notch on its way over the mountains. Hikers can follow original parts of this ancient Native American trail. Head over to the Mahican-Mohawk Trail in Shelburne Falls. Or visit lovely Lookout Mountain in the Mohawk Trail State Forest.

Notchview Reservation in Windsor overlooks the notch carved by the Westfield River. Be adventurous and try one of Notchview's ghost-town hikes! Explore stone walls and cellar holes from an abandoned 1800s settlement. In the winter, try *skijoring*—cross-country skiing with your dog.

Photo: Eastward view from Mount Greylock

N is also for Naumkeag, newspaper, Natural Bridge State Park, nepeta (catmint), nuthatch, and newt.

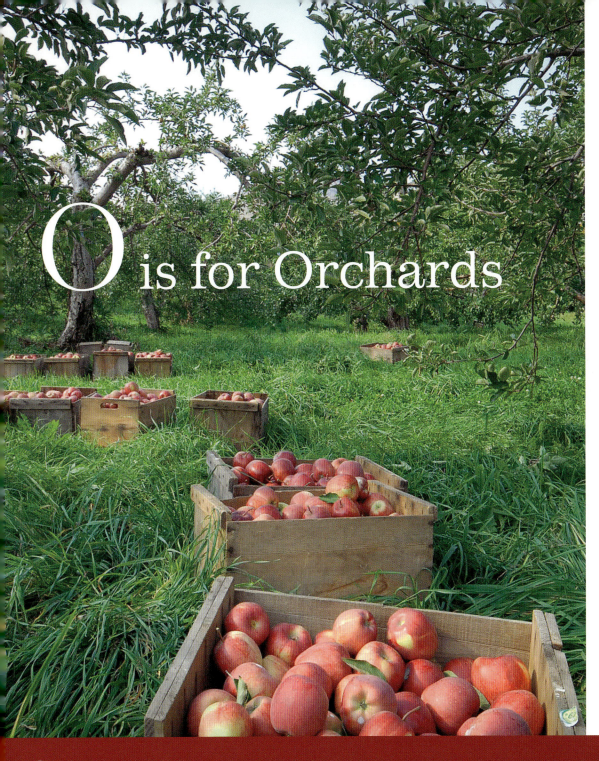

O is for Orchards

*Fruit trees planted
all in a row—
we pick apples,
hanging low.*

Apple trees stand in rows across many Berkshire slopes. Long hours of work keep these orchards in perfect condition. *Orchard growers* prune branches to grow in layers. This allows sunlight and air to reach growing fruit. They also train branches to grow at perfect picking angles. Growers tie some branches up and stake others to the ground. *Orchardists* monitor weather and insects to know when to spray for diseases and bugs.

You can find more than fifty varieties of apples to pick in the Berkshires. You can also find pick-your-own cherry, plum, and pear orchards.

Orchards aren't just for fruit. The Hebert Arboretum in Pittsfield has a seed orchard where volunteers are planting three thousand American chestnut seedlings. These disease-resistant trees will someday shade Berkshire yards.

Photo: Jaeschke's Orchard, Adams

O is also for otters, oaks, oxbows, October Mountain, and Otis Reservoir.

*Pick a pumpkin
from the pile.
It's time to carve
a big-toothed smile!*

Some pumpkins are smooth, while others have warty bumps. You can grow palm-size pumpkins, or ones that weigh more than your family. There are yellow, white, and pink pumpkins. But the classic jack-o'-lantern pumpkin was developed right here in the southern Berkshires, and it's called the Howden pumpkin.

John Howden introduced his famous pumpkin in 1971. Most plant breeders spread pollen by hand, but Howden let bees do the job. Year after year, he saved seeds from his best pumpkins. He later developed the forty-two-pound Howden Biggie from a single, giant pumpkin—a natural mistake (or *mutation*). His son, Bruce Howden, continues to develop new varieties.

Howden Farm in Sheffield has thousands of pick-your-own pumpkins. You can also find twenty-five-pound Howden pumpkins at farm stands and grocery stores across the country.

P is for Pumpkins

P is also for picnics, parades, plays, potters, porcupines, and Pontoosuc Lake.

Q is for Quarry

*Workers cut
the hillside rocks,
slicing nature's
building blocks.*

The Berkshires are rich in rocks. Shallow seas once covered the area, but mountain-building forces and ancient volcanoes changed the landscape half a billion years ago. What was once below water transformed into limestone, marble, granite, soapstone, schist, and slate.

Workers have harvested these rocks from hillside quarries for hundreds of years. Berkshire marble is part of the US Capitol, the Senate, and the Lincoln Memorial in Washington, D.C. Quarries throughout the area still provide gravel and rock for buildings, tombstones, walkways, and more.

Many old quarries have closed, but you can explore the abandoned marble quarry near the Natural Bridge in North Adams. Or visit the historic Becket granite quarry to see the rusted remains of trucks, sheds, and a derrick used long ago.

Photo: Natural Bridge State Park, North Adams

Q is also for Questing (reservation in New Marlborough), quartzite, quilts, and quirky art.

R is for Race

Area athletic clubs host dozens of races throughout the year. Many races are fund-raisers for research, scholarships, or local charities. Food and live music often accompany these events.

Warm weather sees an explosion of foot, bike, and boat races. Some trail races loop through remote areas in state parks. Canoeists and kayakers shoot the Westfield River rapids. When snow arrives, the competitive spirit heats up. Snowshoers and skiers take over the racing scene.

Families challenge themselves in mountain bike races at Springside Park in Pittsfield. Balance-beam and wheelie contests add to the fun. Cheer for your favorite team in the Raft Guide Olympics at the Deerfield River Fest, or root for Thunderbolt racers as they ski up Mount Greylock.

Photo: Josh Billings RunAground triathlon, Stockbridge Bowl, Great Barrington

R is also for resorts, Rockwell Museum, Ragged Mountain, ravines, Red Bat Cave, and ribbon snakes.

S is for Syrup

*Boil the sap
to make syrup, please,
such sweet treats
from maple trees.*

Making maple syrup has come a long way. Four hundred years ago, Native Americans collected sap in hollowed-out logs and then dropped hot rocks in the sap. This boiled away the water, leaving sugar behind.

Today, maple farmers in the Berkshires use buckets or miles of tubing to collect sap. They boil off the water in big, flat pans in sugarhouses. Researchers recently found a new way to harvest sap that saves time and conserves land. Farmers will be able to plant rows of saplings in small fields, then cut and cap the young trees with plastic bags to collect the sap.

Maple syrup isn't just for pancakes. It's also used in recipes for desserts and meat sauces. You can even find maple syrup recipes for tacos, beets, and Brussels sprouts!

Photo: Rob Leab, Ioka Valley Farm, Hancock

S is also for Shakers, sheep, steeples, stone walls, skunk cabbage, and snowshoes.

*Music magic
comes from the Shed.
Haunting notes
soar overhead.*

Tanglewood is the summer home of the Boston Symphony Orchestra. Pack a picnic and join thousands on the estate's lawn in Lenox. There's music for everyone at the world-famous Tanglewood Music Festival.

Gifted high school musicians thrive at the Boston University Tanglewood Institute (BUTI). It's the only such program associated with a major orchestra. Students soak in local history during their music-filled summer. Talented young artists work closely with mentors. They watch their role models play with the BSO, and perform their own series of concerts. They may even meet guest soloists, like violinist Joshua

Bell and cello player Yo-Yo Ma.

In 2014, BUTI students had a surprise guest. A bear broke into their kitchen and pigged out on ice cream! This unexpected visitor was nicknamed Lenny Bear, in honor of the famous composer and conductor Leonard Bernstein, who delighted Tanglewood audiences for years.

Photo: The Shed, Tanglewood, Lenox

T is for Tanglewood

T is also for theater, totems, Tannery Falls, Taconic Mountains, trails, turkeys, and tadpoles.

U is for Upside Down

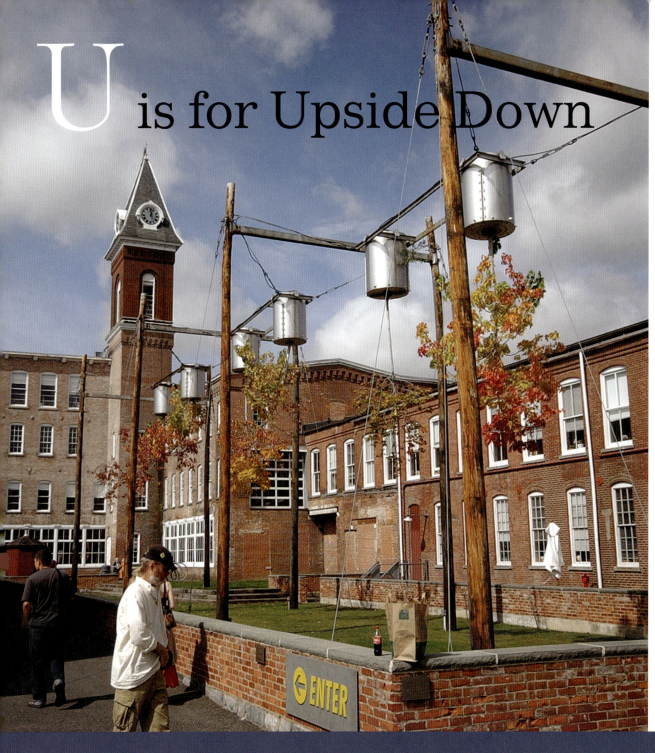

Upside-down trees make us stop and stare. Why are they hanging up in the air?

Yes, believe your eyes! Upside-down, living trees greet visitors at MASS MoCA, a museum in North Adams that is dedicated to modern art. Natalie Jeremijenko's *Tree Logic* is art in slow motion. The trees change over time as branches reach for the sun. The first generation of upside-down trees retired in 2007. They now thrive right side up in a field at the Clark Art Institute in Williamstown.

Contemporary art dares us to think, question, and wonder—and so does science.

In 1895, geologist Daniel Clark studied Tyringham Cobble. At this geologic wonder in Tyringham, older rock layers rested on younger ones. Clark believed the upside-down hill had tumbled off a nearby mountain. Wrong! Scientists now know that movement in the earth's crust pushed older rocks up and over the younger layers.

Photo: ***Tree Logic,*** Massachusetts Museum of Contemporary Art, North Adams

U is also for Upper Housatonic Valley African American Heritage Trail, understudy, and uplands.

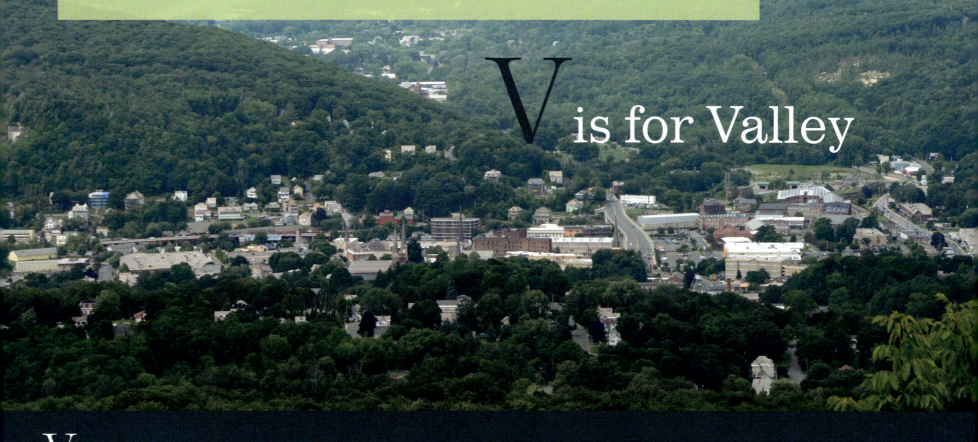

*Tucked between mountains
where wide rivers flow,
towns spread out
in valleys below.*

Mile-thick glaciers scraped through the Berkshires thousands of years ago. They carved out broad, U-shaped valleys. When the glaciers retreated, they left valley floors buried in gravel and clay. Glacial lakes deposited a top layer of rich soil and organic debris. When these giant lakes drained, they left behind fertile land for settlers. Towns sprang up in these isolated valleys.

These small cities and towns offer a blend of inspiring, historic, and quirky places to visit. Explore hundreds of galleries filled with work by local artisans. Grab lunch at the historic Red Lion Inn, in Stockbridge, which has served guests since the 1700s. Visit quaint shops in Pittsfield, North Adams, and Great Barrington. What one-of-a-kind treasure will *you* find?

Photo: North Adams

V is for Valley

V is also for Ventfort Hall, vernal pools, vegetation, vineyards, verbena (flower), veery (bird), and vulture.

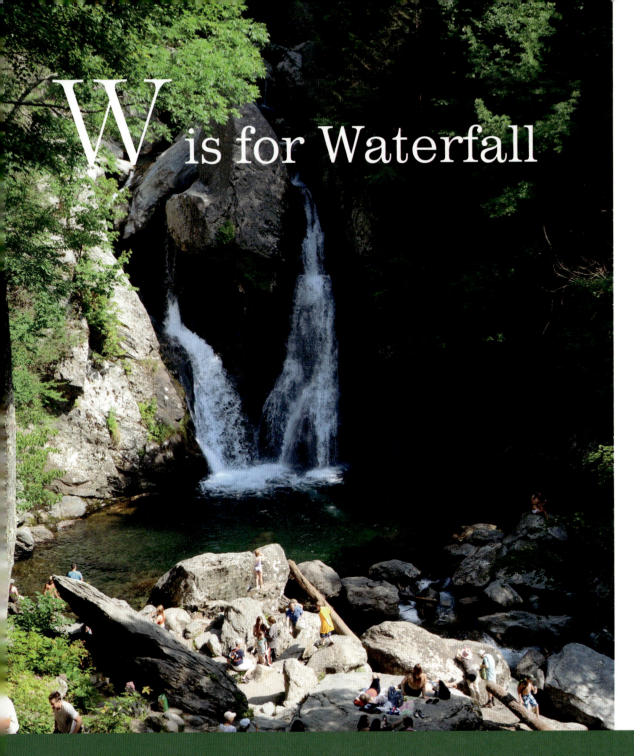

W is for Waterfall

*Water tumbles
down to a pool.
Its splashing mist
keeps us cool.*

Berkshire waterfalls change with the seasons. They thunder down slopes, fed by snowmelt in the spring. During warm summer months, they may slip around moss-covered rocks. And winter waterfalls quietly gurgle behind curtains of ice.

Bash Bish Falls, in Mount Washington State Forest, is the most photographed waterfall in the area. It cuts through a gorge, plunging sixty feet into a deep pool. Legends of Mahican maidens falling to their death surround the falls. There are even tales of Indian treasure buried nearby.

Follow in Henry David Thoreau's famous footsteps. He often hiked to The Cascade near North Adams. Or head for the swimming hole below Umpachene Falls in New Marlborough. Explore the many personalities of Glendale Falls in Middlefield as it bounds 150 feet down rocky ledges.

Photo: Bash Bish Falls, Mount Washington State Forest

W is also for wilderness, wetlands, whitewater rafting, Whitcomb Summit, and Williams College.

X is for Xeriscape

*No rain in sight,
but that's okay—
my plants are
blooming anyway!*

Xeriscape (ZEER-i-scape) landscape designs reduce water usage. But they aren't dry. They aren't boring. They put the right plant in the right spot. Many parks and gardens in the Berkshires use Xeriscape techniques to conserve water and reduce labor.

The average-size lawn needs 10,000 gallons of water a year to stay green. Create a Xeriscape design to reduce water use by up to 60 percent, replacing part of your lawn with patios, walkways, and mulched garden areas.

Gardeners using fancy, nonnative plants may discover they are a lot of work. These pretty plants may not even survive in local conditions. That's why Xeriscape gardeners often use native plants in their landscape plans to create natural habitats. These plants don't mind hot, dry spells, and do just fine with local rainfall—no extra watering needed!

Photo: Berkshire Botanical Garden, West Stockbridge

X is also for xerophyte (water-conserving plant), xanthophyll (leaf pigment), and xylograph (wood engraving).

Y is for Yarn

*Afghans, hats,
and fuzzy socks
are sheared and spun
from local flocks.*

Animal coats have many names: fleece, wool, down, fur, or hair. The fibers in these coats are processed and spun into yarn.

Sheep and alpacas are the most popular fiber animals in the Berkshires. Alpacas come in three hundred shades of natural color!

Local fiber artists create soft mohair yarn from curly-haired angora goats. They also raise llamas and angora rabbits. Sometimes they'll pluck and spin angora yarn while the bunnies snuggle on their laps. They buy yak, camel, and other fibers to add to their stash.

In the Berkshires, you'll find many shops with yarn and knitted and woven goods. Explore Hancock Shaker Village in Pittsfield. Experiment on their spinning wheel and loom. Try dyeing yarn with local plants. Make a drop spindle from a CD, or spin your own pet's hair!

Photo: Yarn, Hancock Shaker Village

Y is also for yoga, yogurt, Yokun Ridge, yoke, yellowthroats, yarrow, and yucca.

Z is for Zip Line

Clipped onto a cable,
we're ready to fly.
We zip through the trees,
feet touching the sky.

Zip lines are treetop trails. Zip-line tours started about twenty years ago in Central and South America, providing a new way to see the forests. A company called Zoar Outdoor introduced this adventure sport to the Berkshires in 2009. Since then, many local ski areas have added zip lines to their summer parks.

More than a hundred zip lines on two dozen courses offer something for everyone. A section of the Valley Jump zip-line tour at Berkshire East in Charlemont is a half-mile long and almost two hundred feet above the ground! Some courses have guides; others are self-guided. Families and friends conquer new challenges as they explore together. These trails in the sky can feature ladders, platforms, rappels, nets, bridges, and dual racing zip lines.

Photo: Brian Boudreau, Northern Berkshire Youth ROPES (Respecting Other People Encouraging Self-Esteem) Program, Historic Valley Campground, Windsor Lake, North Adams

Z is also for Zucchini Festival, Zoar Gap, and Zylonite (the town).

Author photo by Anthony DiChello.

Photo courtesy of Gillian Jones.

ABOUT THE AUTHOR

An explorer at heart, Joannie Duris enjoys discovering new places tucked away in the corners of New England. Her philosophy: Go slow, so you don't miss the good stuff. She studied geology before moving on to a career in nursing. In the winter, she explores the outdoors while helping skiers and snowshoers as a member of the Northfield Mountain Nordic Ski Patrol. She has had stories and articles published in several national children's magazines, and on BoomWriter, a writing website for kids. She leads a local Society of Children's Book Writers and Illustrators (SCBWI) critique group of fellow writers. A New England transplant, Joannie spent much of her childhood in Japan. She lives in central Massachusetts with her husband and three spoiled cats, where she can occasionally be seen chasing black bears away from her bird feeders. Learn more at www.joanduris.com.

ABOUT THE PHOTOGRAPHER

Gillian Jones is a staff photographer for *The Berkshire Eagle*. She was the chief photographer of the *North Adams Transcript*, a daily newspaper, for more than twenty years, until early 2014. Her work appears nationally through the Associated Press. She also teaches photography courses at the Massachusetts College of Liberal Arts and serves as an adviser to the school's weekly newspaper, *The Beacon*, where she got her start as a student photojournalist. Originally from Long Island, New York, she has lived in North Adams and called the Berkshires home since the early 1980s. Find out more at www.photosbygillian.com.

ALSO PUBLISHED BY ISLANDPORT PRESS

C is for Cape Cod

Written by Christina Laurie

Photographs by Steve Heaslip

A is for Acadia

Written by Ruth Gortner Grierson

Photographs by Richard Johnson

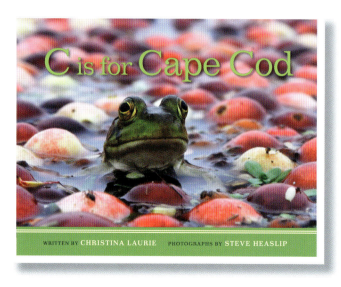

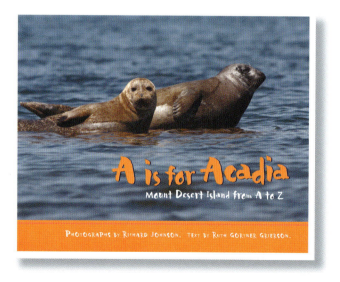